June 14, 1897, Aurora, Wyoming

My Dear Professor Osborn:

Wish you were here to enjoy the pleasure of taking out those beautiful black, perfect bones, also to eat some of the juicy antelope steak I got Sunday.

Very sincerely yours,
Barnum Brown

June 25, 1902

My dear Brown:

Judging from your report, you are in . . . "Holy ground"; and there is every reason to think that by careful inquiry among the natives, by making friends wherever you can, and by energetic prospecting you may find something of real value.

Always sincerely yours,
Prof. Osborn

August 12, 1902, camp on Hell Creek, Montana

My Dear Professor Osborn:

Quarry No. 1 contains the . . . bones of a large Carnivorous Dinosaur . . . I have never seen anything like it.

Sincerely yours,
Barnum Brown

June 24, 1905, camp on Hell Creek, Montana

My Dear Professor Osborn:

Yesterday we struck a concretion containing a large skull bone and today found another . . . Please send me ½ doz. short heavy chisels of best steel . . . also doz. crooked awls without handles.

Sincerely yours,
Barnum Brown

July 8, 1908, Camp Big Dry Creek, Montana

My Dear Professor Osborn:

At last I have some good news to report. I made a ten strike last week finding fifteen [tail vertebrae] connected . . . We have . . . moved camp to the specimen and borrowed scraper and plow for a big cutting.

Very sincerely yours,
Barnum Brown

July 30, 1908

My dear Brown:

I congratulate you with all my heart on this splendid discovery.

Yours very sincerely,
Professor Osborn

To my wonderful writing group:
Mary Atkinson, Jacqueline Davies,
Sarah Lamstein, and Carol Peacock
—T.F.

For Kate O.
—B.K.

BARNUM'S BONES

*How Barnum Brown Discovered
the Most Famous Dinosaur in the World*

Tracey Fern   Pictures by Boris Kulikov

Margaret Ferguson Books / Farrar Straus Giroux / New York

Something exciting happened in Carbondale, Kansas, on February 12, 1873. The Brown family had a baby boy. It was even more exciting than the circus, and the Browns adored the circus! In fact, the Browns loved the circus so much they named their baby Barnum, after the most famous circus owner in America, P. T. Barnum. They hoped Barnum's important-sounding, unusual name would inspire him to do important, unusual things.

Barnum started doing something unusual right from the start.

As soon as Barnum could toddle, he followed along behind his pa's plow, plucking up the ancient corals and clams and snails and scallops that it unearthed.

Barnum filled boxes with his fossil collection. He filled his dresser with his collection. He filled his entire bedroom with his collection. When he filled the front parlor, his mama—who had never considered that the important, unusual things she had dreamed of for her son would involve fossil shellfish in the parlor—made him move his treasures out to the laundry house.

Barnum spent years studying his collection, trying to imagine what the world must have been like millions of years ago, when his family's high, dry farm was at the bottom of a shallow, swirling sea. Then one day he read about dinosaur fossils that had been unearthed in the West—*Brontosaurus* and *Triceratops* and *Stegosaurus* and more! Barnum longed to find some bones for himself, especially bones from species that no one had ever found before.

Barnum got his chance when he took a course in paleontology at the University of Kansas. He was such a good student that his professor invited him to spend the summers of 1894 and 1895 on fossil hunts in South Dakota and Wyoming. Each morning, Barnum set out at sunrise. He hiked over mountains, across creek beds, down precipices, through streams, and around rattlesnake nests. Most folks would think this was torture. Barnum thought it was wonderful.

Barnum, who was an unusually nice dresser, sometimes went prospecting in a fur coat, a suit and tie, buffed black boots, and a bowler hat. No matter how he was dressed, Barnum found bones. He didn't discover any new species, but he and the rest of the Wyoming expedition collected more than 1,400 pounds of bones— including a six-foot-long, four-and-a-half-foot-wide, nearly perfect *Triceratops* skull!

Henry Fairfield Osborn, a professor at Columbia University and an administrator at the American Museum of Natural History in New York City, heard about Barnum's talent for bone hunting from Barnum's professor at the University of Kansas.

Professor Osborn wanted the museum to have the best dinosaur collection in the world. So far, the museum had none.

Professor Osborn hired Barnum to work on fossil hunts for the museum. Most people called the slightly terrifying Professor Osborn "sir."

Barnum called him "My Dear Professor" because he loved bones as much as Barnum did.

My Dear Professor sent Barnum back to Wyoming in 1897 to hunt fossils. Once again, Barnum didn't discover any new species, but he did unearth the museum's first important dinosaurs—two enormous long-necked sauropods, a *Diplodocus longus* and an *Apatosaurus*.

Then, in December 1898, My Dear Professor sent Barnum on a collecting trip to Patagonia, in South America. Barnum found four and a half tons of mammal fossils, despite being shipwrecked and nearly eaten by a mountain lion. More than a year later, he returned to New York City with his boatload of bones.

"He must be able to smell fossils," My Dear Professor said.

Barnum had more than just a good nose. He pored over maps and geology books. He chatted with local people. He studied the shape and color and texture of the rock layers. His passion for fossils led him to uncover more and more bones, but he still dreamed of discovering something new.

One morning in 1902, Barnum's friend William Hornaday, the director of the New York Zoological Park, gave Barnum an interesting rock that he had found on a hunting trip in the badlands near Hell Creek, Montana. Barnum's nose started twitching. The rock wasn't just any rock—it was the horn of a *Triceratops*!

In June 1902, Barnum and a small crew headed by train and then by horses to the badlands. Barnum found lots of fossils, but they were all damaged or familiar. Back in New York, My Dear Professor was getting cranky.

His rivals at the Carnegie Museum of Natural History in Pittsburgh had made an exciting find—many bones from a new species of dinosaur, a *Diplodocus carnegii*. It was named after Andrew Carnegie, a businessman and the founder of the museum.

One day Barnum spotted some boulders that had tumbled down a steep cliff. He scrambled off his horse and up the cliff. He found a bone the color of milky coffee sticking out of the hillside. Barnum swooshed away loose sand with a soft brush. Then he started digging around the bone with his pick. The deeper he dug, the more bone he found. Barnum dug until night fell.

The next morning he returned with his crew and they dug until they hit a layer of flinty blue sandstone nearly as hard as steel. Barnum carefully blasted off layers of rock with dynamite. Then the quarry filled with the metallic pings of hammers, the scraping of awls against bone, and the soft whisper of brushes.

Finally, Barnum began to see the outline of a massive curving bone—a dinosaur's pelvis. Then he uncovered a few of the creature's backbones, a thighbone, an arm bone, and other fragments. Barnum had never seen anything like these bones before.

Unfortunately, by early October, the season was over. Soon snow would cover the badlands. Barnum had to get his fragile bones safely to the museum. He painted shellac on the exposed parts of the bones, covered the shellac with a thin layer of newspaper, and slathered on layers of plaster-soaked burlap strips to form a hard, protective cast around the fossils.

Barnum hitched four horses to a wagon and slowly pulled the two-ton pelvis and other bones 130 miles back to the train. Along the way, Barnum couldn't resist collecting some interesting leaves and what he thought might be four ancient crocodile skeletons, too.

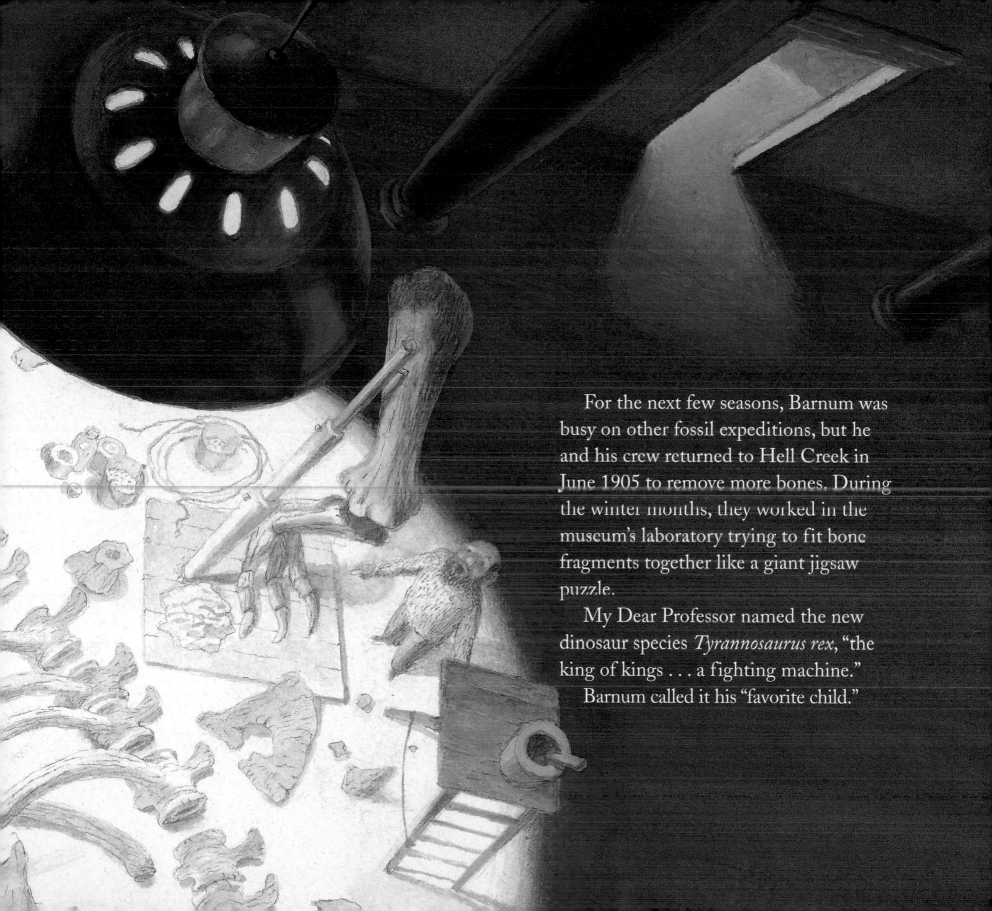

For the next few seasons, Barnum was busy on other fossil expeditions, but he and his crew returned to Hell Creek in June 1905 to remove more bones. During the winter months, they worked in the museum's laboratory trying to fit bone fragments together like a giant jigsaw puzzle.

My Dear Professor named the new dinosaur species *Tyrannosaurus rex*, "the king of kings . . . a fighting machine." Barnum called it his "favorite child."

Barnum and My Dear Professor studied the *T. rex* bone fragments and even displayed a portion of the skeleton in the museum, but many pieces of the *T. rex* puzzle were missing, including the complete head. Barnum longed to know more about his new dinosaur. What exactly did it look like? What did it eat? How did it walk?

So in 1908, Barnum and a few men went to an area of the badlands that he had never searched before. Barnum looked for weeks and collected nothing but sunburn and mosquito bites.

On July 1, Barnum and his horse Brownie were clip-clopping along Big Dry Creek after another long, hot, fruitless day of prospecting. Barnum had already combed this area several times. He knew he should start looking somewhere else, but somehow he smelled fossils. He scanned the buttes one last time. Suddenly, Barnum saw an unusual rock glinting in the sun.

Barnum and Brownie clambered up the butte for a closer look. Yes! Just as Barnum had hoped, the unusual rock was the smooth, rounded end of a bone! But what exactly was it?

The next day, Barnum and his crew dug a six-foot trench around the bone. They found bones everywhere. But the bones were too jumbled and too deeply embedded in the sandstone to identify.

Barnum scraped and plowed and dug and blasted for weeks and still did not know what he had found. To make matters worse, he couldn't find any additional men to help make the digging—or the cooking—go faster. Luckily, Barnum was an unusually good cook.

Slowly, Barnum uncovered enough bones to identify his find. It was the treasure he had dreamed of—a perfect, four-foot-long *T. rex* skull, studded with serrated six-inch-long teeth. In fact, the whole skeleton was nearly perfect, with only the leg bones missing. Together with his first find, he finally had enough bones to piece together the entire animal.

Barnum, who was an unusually good dancer, celebrated his find
at a nearby ranch by doing the tango and the two-step until midnight.
My Dear Professor was so excited that he decided
to come to Montana to visit the *T. rex* himself.

It took Barnum until October 1908 to dig up all the bones and haul them by horse and wagon to the nearest train. Then it took seven more years to clean and mount the skeleton.

At last, Barnum could see what he had dreamed about for so long: the complete skeleton of an entirely new dinosaur species—and a whopping big one too! Barnum's new flesh-eating dinosaur was 47 feet long, with huge feet and sharp claws.

T. rex quickly became the most famous dinosaur in the world. Millions of visitors came to see it. Hundreds of scientists came to study it.

Barnum went on to collect bones all over the world. He hunted by raft in Canada,

by elephant in India,

by airplane in the United States,

and by diving in Cuba.
    Barnum collected more dinosaur bones than anyone on earth. But *T. rex* was still his favorite child.

Just as his family had wanted, Barnum did something important and unusual:
he discovered a sleeping dinosaur and brought it back to life.

Sixty-six million years after extinction, *T. rex* lives on in Barnum's bones.

Author's Note

When Barnum Brown arrived at the American Museum of Natural History in 1897, it did not have a single dinosaur specimen. When he died in 1963, the museum had the largest collection of dinosaur bones in the world. Barnum had unearthed most of these himself. Barnum also collected fossils of other extinct animals, including fish, mammals, and invertebrates, as well as living plants and archaeological objects.

Barnum searched for bones on every continent except Antarctica. He was an unusually good storyteller and had a tale to tell about every bone hunt—a run-in with a giant spider in India, a fall into a volcanic crater in New Mexico, and a bout with malaria that somehow led to his collecting a complete fossil aardvark, some fossilized ancient horses, and three hundred species of living wildflowers!

In addition to hunting bones, Barnum had another job: spy. During World War I and World War II, Barnum used his job as a fossil hunter to obtain important geological and geographic information for the United States.

Barnum and his favorite child, *T. rex*, at the Museum of Natural History, ca. 1918

Although Barnum was a great fossil finder, he often didn't write down details about his discoveries in field notes or publish as many scientific papers as his colleagues. Similarly, although Barnum wrote some unpublished autobiographical notes that included family lore about his naming and also told other people tales about his early family life, he never published an autobiography. As a result, some aspects of his early life—for example, which of his family members were circus fans and exactly when and why Barnum developed his unusual habit of sometimes dressing formally in the field—are unclear. Despite these occasionally incomplete or contradictory details, Barnum's fossil discoveries speak for themselves. They are still used today to try to answer major questions in paleontology, and some of Barnum's beliefs, including the then much-debated theory that birds and dinosaurs may be related, have been widely accepted.

His techniques, discoveries, and ideas continue to help us understand the time when dinosaurs—especially Barnum's favorite child, *T. rex*—truly were the kings of the earth.